Raingatherer

Franklin Brainard

ACKNOWLEDGMENTS

I wish to thank the editors of the following magazines for permission to reprint these poems, sometimes revised since their first appearances.

BLACK FLAG: The Wave I Hear Is Light.

CAFÉ SOLO: Because My Horses Wait.

EPOS: Pö Chu-i's Poem.

THE HIRAM POETRY REVIEW: Inland Sea.

THE MIDWEST QUARTERLY: In And Out; The Stove Leaks Light.

THE NORTH STONE REVIEW: Song for a Widow's Marriage; Roubaix Cemetery; Pressing Slotted Marks; Dry Summers Never Leave; poem 1 of the Candling; My Mother; My Father; Dickinson, North Dakota; Another Will Build His Fence; I Reap the Summer's Fallowing.

PERSPECTIVE: Raingatherer.

STEELHEAD: Log House; poems 2 and 3 of The Candling.

TODAY'S HEALTH, published by The American Medical Association: White Ropes.

Published and distributed by
Minnesota Writers' Publishing House
21 Ridge Road
Morris, Minnesota 56267

Cover Drawing by Franz Richter

ISBN 0-913894-00-1

For Muriel, Judith, Mark, and Beth

A CONVERSATION

Two young Minnesota poets, Mike Kincaid and James Naiden, had a conversation with Franklin Brainard at his house in New Brighton, on December 5th 1971. Some excerpts from the conversation follow. The whole interview may be read in *The North Stone Review,* No. 3.

Naiden: You said you've written poems for how long?

Brainard: Well, seriously I've probably written since I was nineteen years of age.

Naiden: That's over thirty years—

Brainard: Yeah.

Naiden: And it took you how long to get published?

Brainard: Twenty-five.

Naiden: Twenty-five years—what does that mean to you, that long?

Brainard: Well, it means that I wasn't sending out enough and it means that I wasn't good enough—and, you know, a poem has to stand the letter test: your voice and your personality and everything that you are is not there in the editor's office. And what he has is a piece of paper— but he may have a hangover and his wife may have given him a bad time and he may be reading the poem at eight o'clock in the morning. I mean, you have to speak to his sensibilities at this time and—

Kincaid: Editors are like that.

Brainard: Well, we're all like that. I don't object to the fact that it took twenty-five years, but at this stage of the game I'd like to get a hearing—there is *that* thing.

Naiden: So it's been the past six or seven years since you've been publishing poetry?

Brainard: The very first things were published in 1965—and I figured that I had been writing for twenty-five years seriously, preceding that. I mean, I wrote while I was on merchant ships —I was *always* writing. But I wasn't getting close to experience, somehow or another. If you'd look at some of the first things that I published, like "That Bag Of Winds" in the Chicago *Jewish Forum,* you'd see complicated, involuted, compacted lines. Now, I've gotten to the stage where I can say things—fairly complicated things—in fairly simple language—which of course is what I've been aiming for. But I didn't know what I was aiming for at the time, but now I realize that this is the thing that I should have been aiming for.

5

Naiden: You mentioned Ray Smith . . .

Brainard: Oh, Ray Smith is a marvelous poet, and I mentioned Ray —first, I suppose,—because he was the first poet I met. I met him in the spring of '65. Matter of fact, I think probably Ray and Mike Kincaid met just shortly after Ray and I met. But I had to be forty-five years old, and I had to have written in an almost kind of sensibility vacuum for years before I met anybody with whom I could communicate; and here was a fine, sensitive man who was so quiet that you had to draw his poems from him. But he would take yours and take them and look at them with love and with kindness and would help—it was a new experience for me.

Naiden: You live in New Brighton now, in 1971, but could you tell us something about your earlier life? What brought you to this point in your creative work, as well as in your own life?

Brainard: Well, I think—I think I was hooked on the American Dream for a while, and while, at some level while Muriel and I and the children were living in a log house in the Black Hills—we lived there in the timber for eight years—at some level I knew that this was one of the great periods of my life, just as a living experience, I couldn't quite make a living at one job, always had to work at something else.

Naiden: When did you come here?

Brainard: Well, we came down here in 1956 from Deadwood, South Dakota.

Naiden: And you had lived there previously—

Brainard: We'd lived there for nine years, one in an apartment and eight in the timber—yeah, it was marvelous—

Naiden: But, prior to 1956, you lived in the Dakotas all your life?

Brainard: Yeah, well it was before, living in South Dakota in the Black Hills, I'd lived in North Dakota . . . One of my poems about the Heart River was published in the *Hornbook Magazine* . . . The Heart River is a river near Dickinson . . .

Naiden: You've been in Minnesota for how long?

Brainard: Fifteen years.

Naiden: Fifteen years. And I suppose you've seen a lot of Minnesota poets, you've met some of them. What aspect of this area— the Upper Midwest—is most important for a poet's experience and life?

Brainard: I suppose I could mention John Caddy's close observation of reptilian life. He had a magnificent poem about a frog and its eyes, and he has a wonderful poem about the asininity of modern civilization and the Indian in that modern civilization, and the Leroys out shooting on Sundays with their rifles. And there's a wonderful poem by the black poet, Roy McBride, which grows out of his observation of the American scene from the Middle West—and that's "Levi Strauss, You Have Left Your Mark on The Ass

6

of America." You see, many of the things that these poets have here is a physical observation of the earth and its spirit for them and its philosophy for them and so on. And you can't shut this out, even in the middle of town—like some of Mike Kincaid's things deal with the birds on the branches on the trees outside his window—and its not the old Victorian birds-and-bees thing, in any sense, it's always part of this human probe of who are we and where are we and where have we come from and what heaven is ours, if at all?

Kincaid: Now there's a feeling I get from your poetry—the agate reminded me of it—the very fine sense of contour and process and texture that goes on in your best poems. It relates to the crystalline structure of a rock or the taste of metal or how a branch grows or something like that—it's very primary.

Brainard: Well, you know, it's a funny thing. I think a lot of that stuff grew out of my dad. He was a country lawyer—and he used to say that his business depended upon the farmer, and if the farmer wouldn't make it, *he* wouldn't make it. And always he was taking me around, all through North Dakota. I can remember rattling around in his Model T Ford, and we used to go across the Missouri River at points where there were ferries and not bridges, and he was always showing me things. Like—he didn't give me any lectures on it, I mean, he'd make sure that there were things that I could see—and, oh, in a similar vein, when I was nine years old, in 1929, he took me through East St. Louis so that I could have a look at a ghetto. He never gave me a lecture, never said a word, but he just took me, driving slowly. And he was a poet himself. He didn't ever write a poem that I know of—but we'd go by a graveyard and he'd say something that sounded like it might have come from Sir Thomas Browne, but I never was able to find it in Sir Thomas Browne, and I finally concluded that it was his own thing; but we'd go by a graveyard and he'd say to me: "The cities of the dead are larger than the cities of the living." And this is the way he spoke.

Naiden: I suppose he's deceased now?

Brainard: Yes, he died in '41.

Naiden: I know my own father's influence—he's still living—but my relationship with him has been an influence in a lot of my creative work. I suppose your father's was to you.

Brainard: Oh, yes, my father—and my mother, too. My mother was one of those delightful products of the post-Freudian, post-Darwinian world, and she was very scientific on the surface. But she'd go round the kitchen and she'd be baking her bread and she'd recite: "So live that when thy summons come to join that innumerable caravan . . ." or "Whither midst falling dew . . ." or something of this nature. So both of them were contributing language—and my dad was a keen observer. We were going by a farm one time and he said, "You see that water tank over there, son? Describe to me what you see." And what happened was that you had these metal bands around these wooden water tanks, and when they dried out, the parts separated. And they had fallen down inward toward the center of the circle. I said to him: "It fell apart." Now he said: "The German farmer, looking at that, would say: "It fell together." And that's much more accurate . . .

Naiden: How old are you now? Fifty-two?
Brainard: I'll be fifty-two in June.

SONG FOR A WIDOW'S MARRIAGE

Husband, I come to you, no girl,
but a woman earthed from North Dakota.
I have known the farm,
have milked cows,
have forked manure
into the spreader,
have smelt the deep ammonia
of horse urine.
I have borne the womb burden;
I have borne and bear
the woes of children,
woes that hang as unaccountable
as moon dogs or a dry dipper.
I come to you no girl
but I come rich
with peasant blood
and warm as sun-dug potatoes.
You shall have me warm beside you
when winter turns over the roof's edge;
you shall have me
like something held for winter
coming live with flavor
from the double-doored root cellar;
and, when I take the pies
from the oven
and when I take the bread
that yeasted all the kitchen
in the afternoon,
come, kiss my neck
and walk with me
through the late garden.

ROUBAIX CEMETERY

I have looked at the Roubaix Cemetery:
its pines have fallen from another world,
have caught a mountainside
to hold the rupture and the carving of an age
while eating it slowly.

When sun comes the earth is speckled
like the breast of a grouse,
the columns of created light
carrying dust older and finer than soil.

I have looked into the Roubaix Cemetery
where bones of the Finlanders lie
undertaker straight,
boxed against the raw half soil
and rawer stones.

Their passions are somewhere else
dancing;
their old hands that grew to tools
no longer milk,
no longer turn the separator;
their madness no longer asks them, "Why?"

Let me lie there.
I shall leave the troubles of my marrow,
shall leave my madness,
shall leave the loves I've ruptured,
and, in the grouse light,
climb the columns of dust
and disappear in sun.

THE STOVE LEAKS LIGHT

The log house warms
and as it warms the flies come to.
Stirred by aspen warmth
they gather at sunlit windows.

An unexpected summer turns them on.
Had we not come
they would have waited for a warmer sun,
a sun that pressures seed in loam.

What season is it that we grow?
My wife says forest flies will wake
in spring though they freeze in snow.
Is it true or old wives' tale?

At night they settle around
the latest warmth:
the last light left on,
the cracks in bricks about the hearth.

We lie in bed—
my wife, heavy and warm with sleep,
my head
keeping count over strange sheep.

The night turns night
and I turn thoughts and eyes;
the stove leaks light
on sleeping, winter-wakened flies.

RAINGATHERER

I have said, "Dear God," under my breath a thousand times.
Rolling I have wrapped the thousand night sheets around the days
I could not reach, could not hold.
Each day is just beyond my fingers:
my madness, my family's madness, the world's.
Our Father have mercy on us who gather rain.
Our Father have mercy on me
one of these the least of Your raingatherers.
In a world of earthenware I come with a paper cup.

PŎ CHU-I'S POEM

This morning I read Pŏ Chui-i's poem,
"The Red Cockatoo,"
read Arthur Waley's translation
one of the bars in my cage being
that I can not read Chinese.
It made me think of all the bars
for all our cages:
war,
sickness,
my black friends in Stillwater Prison,
my disturbed self,
my disturbed children,
my wife going quietly to work,
my going quietly to work
when all there is is work.

Up the mountain side
the deer step on stonecrop;
something yellow dies.
Up the air
the uncaged insects fly;
up the air
the swallows swoop them in
and something waits
for sudden birds.

Peace, peace and there is no peace.
Love, love and there is no love.

All them talks about freedom
ain't goin' there
freedom

We grow quiet in work.

By the sweat of your souls
ye shall . . .

The words sweat.

The galled horse
grows white hair upon the gall.

There is honey in the dead lion's head.

PRESSING SLOTTED MARKS

The highland ox, ring in nose,
his horns an almost quarter moon,
moves forward step by folding step
straighter than any prancing horse.
He carries his weight
and pulls many times himself,
pressing slotted marks in mud.
On mornings when every vein
ropes me to the bed,
I see him, hair hanging,
pulling the load he did not choose.

INLAND SEA

Here in the wind-shave of prairie land
through senses the animal did not think about
I feel the swell of seas
and in my mouth
waking
I taste salt.
My tiredness rises to a breaking.
I shall be coral for an unknown reef
of grass.
I shall be lime to green.
I shall yellow cactus flowers.
Because I live
because I love this living
because this animal would die to live
I'll die to rise again
as seasonal.
I shall be salt for absent Agassiz
lifting now to grass.

IN AND OUT

These rafters—full 2x4's and rough—
have held up sky since 1886,
have braced the lumber that cradles
a slanted chimney.
I see details:
curved saw marks,
the hair of unplaned lumber,
the clinging bat blinking the day away.
I see bricks that would suck water,
the curled edges of mortar pinched out and down.
What escapes me below the salt storms in my blood?
There is a fog I can not see for dark.
Somewhere before the lobes
there is a remote fo'c'sle
and battened in I hear a water spout.
They have never found the agate in my guts
but I feel its layers
and each night the bat goes out to see.

DRY SUMMERS NEVER LEAVE

Dry summers never leave.
Grasshoppers that separated sun from earth
that lived a season
live for the ever of a man.
They hop and fly
consume the crops
lose their shapes in their own buzzing
twist in the oil swirl of sense
until only their compound eyes remain
floating like cells in the blood
keeping watch on the grass of dry summers
keeping watch on the dry stars
keeping watch on brittle trees
keeping watch
on the prairies of the marrow
on the man walking out of himself
to water heaven.

LOG HOUSE

Frost creeps around the rug at the foot of the door.
Outside the snow-rumped horses head downwind.
My pitch fire shakes the stove
and the dark logs warm and dream of being trees.

BECAUSE MY HORSES WAIT

Out to the frozen pump
with a tea kettle of hot water.
I see the white hair
that grows from iron,
keep working until water comes
because, winter muzzles white,
my horses wait.

THE CANDLING
(Four Short Poems)

I

I am candled by a star.
My bones are shadows
in a shadow body.
Substantial things grow thin.
Sun shines through
empty snake skins
twisted in the grass.

II

Is logic the mist
the waking brain
impresses on the sleeping wish?

Dwarves make friends
among short people.

III

Old men take soup
lingering with breast sounds
over the noodles.

IV

When I hear the pre-dawn bellows of cattle
moving between the hills,
I dream of split leaves in mud
trailing to salt and stream
and acorn-hooved deer at the edges of the herd.
Potato vines turn green in the deep sun
I carry from sleep to sleep.

MY MOTHER

When I've held life too close
and been hurt by anthills,
I think of my mother
making bread with vigor,
eating onions though doctors
said she shouldn't,
learning Spanish in her sixties,
hiring out to pick cotton in Texas
because she had to know,
calmly giving herself insulin
no needle too much.
I remember her surface
of logic and science
always breaking in the spring floods.
I look at her paintings:
dog, cow, birds,
lonely humans heaving on the pitch and swell
of dark seas in the late orange light of day.
I remember how she and other women
defeated a senator opposed to women's voting.
I remember her saying,
"It takes guts to live in a tough world."
I remember her saying,
"Talk is cheap; it takes money to buy whiskey."

WHITE ROPES

Yesterday's December rain
turned snow this morning
The wind brought white ropes to hold us
and the cattle and horses turned
in their ancient ritual
to head downwind.
I could have read this
if I wished
as the freezing of life
but this isn't so.
The ranch dog, sheep-white with snow,
will not come in;
his life is outside.
There is an endurance,
with hope,
as perennial and seasonal as grass.
The cattle and horses
paw the snow and browse,
and the dog comes to meet me.
I wonder about my place
in the metaphor,
assume mine is theirs.
I turn in,
thinking of the white storm
in my blood:
leukemia;
turn in
remember horses,
remember cattle,
remember dog,
remember badland cedars

knotting up to sun
in land so dry
no tree should grow.
I turn out again
and you
may have the harvest
of my marrow.

DICKINSON, NORTH DAKOTA

Expanding through its section lines
that small town with the Heart River
on its southside
was a little world
arterial to the big one.

Filipinos, Japanese, East Indians
worked its railroad gangs
brought their worlds to railroad sidings:
strange butterfly kites
above the wheat and sod.

It had its murder
and its murder rumors

its body hunger
and its hungering minds
grasping,
like stub-rooted carrot fingers
long cut from an old man's hand.

As boys we heard about its gangsters
on the lam from St. Paul,
Chicago.

We knew where to buy
its bootleg wine—
35¢ a quart.

We knew the bootlegger
who went to bed in St. Joe's Hospital
each time the FBI accountants arrived.
We knew him later
when he was legit
and worth a million.

It had its lonely black boy
whose manhood
white fathers would not accept
whose scholarship to Tuskegee
was quick in coming.

Its Heart met the Missouri,
the Mississippi, the Gulf,
and we believed in sea fish
in our river.

We knew the family of seven
living on $44 a month
WPA wages
living in a horse barn
turned garage
turned home
made from second hand railroad ties.

We knew the kind of mind
that would make a dance hall
called Baghdad
and import a Bactrian camel
and we felt for Charley,
that camel,
when he lost his battle
with an NP train.

We knew

and after Baghdad dances,
Saturday night,
Hollywood was acted out
in back seats.

Out of the lines of men
gone cold to WPA work,
out of the children
picking coal along the NP tracks,
out of the banked houses,
out of the loneliness of land
that wandered into sky,
with little to believe in,
we believed.

We believed in the ripple of the fish tail
from the many-rivered sea.

ANOTHER WILL BUILD HIS FENCE

I put in cedar posts instead of pitch
and was glad with the more temporary thing.
Each has its grace and strength but I knew
that cedar would see me through.
I've felt at times as if there were
something pompous about a longer impermanence.
I have seen too many monuments of death
whose carvings grow illegible.
In rural graveyards, the single hand
its index finger up, stands
reminding and rum
above the sign, "Gone Home."
Well, manure is a temporary thing
and so are the songs of those who sing
walking behind the spreader
and I take for better
the singing of the folk
who walk and know their walk.
And if my cedar posts become the soil
that holds them and the rusted wires fail,
I know another will build his fence
on the same old heaving ground, sensing
that even where my old posts stand
they will no longer do.

I REAP THE SUMMER'S FALLOWING

For me the poem is a winter thing
except for one or two that come like autumn leaves
born wrong in June
from late and arctic wind.

Come from long prairies
that stretch farm widows lonely,
I am not lonely in the modern sense
for loneliness has been the quilt
in which I turned chin-high to sleep .

In the wing-moan of diving ducks,
I feel the coming snow winds
weaving corner sounds around
each abruptness of my house
and I hibernate to life.

In the movement of the sleepless ice,
in the reverberate echo of its cracking
I reap the summer's fallowing.

THE WAVE I HEAR IS LIGHT

They are not echoes
but more like
whispers
that hark back
along a chain
of neuron-seed-neuron.
The wave I hear
goes back before all heart beats
to pulsing God seed in the life stream.
It whispers of a long gestation
in a womb of rock and salt and water.
It whispers of a radiance
before vertebrates
and because of whispers
I keep trying to find a seam.

MY FATHER

That country lawyer took me with him
in his Model T Ford.
Near Watford City
we crossed the Missouri, T and all,
ferried to the other side.

He always showed me the other side:
men riding the freights
going West, going East, going;
East St. Louis in 1929
holding its groin.

He'd look at a water tank for cattle,
circling bands grown loose and fallen,
wooden members dry and fallen to the center,
"How would you describe that?"

"It's fallen apart."

"The German farmer would say
'It fell together.' "

We went on one-pole fishing trips
and when I'd wonder why . . .
"Because I do not want to take
what I can not give."

Great care with his briefs
in the fastest hunt and peck
on his old L. C. Smith—
justice and law, in that order.

Proud of the then freedom,
he'd point to a farm saying,
"That farmer left the old country
to avoid conscription."

In dry land his language came like a spring
and it was green where he spoke.
Passing a cemetery he'd say,
"The cities of the dead are larger
than the cities of the living."

Once, after tears, I slept
and he came to me in a dream
saying, "I'm all right. Don't worry"–
calm rain on cracked earth.

THE WAY OF MAN
FOR MARTIN BUBER

Come back to the garden.
It is not so much that I was driven out
as that I drove you out.
I capitalized my name
leaving yours in small letters
yet you left me bread in the desert.
I ate in bitterness;
I ate in anger,
the food prepared according to the law
but my teeth closing on my own heart.
I saw two worlds
but it was one
in double vision
from too narrow focus.
The retinal hemorrhage holds sight.
The breaking cells hold life.
The time I divided
moment to moment to death
has lost all tense.
Turning, I let You in.
You are come to the Garden
and it is Ours.